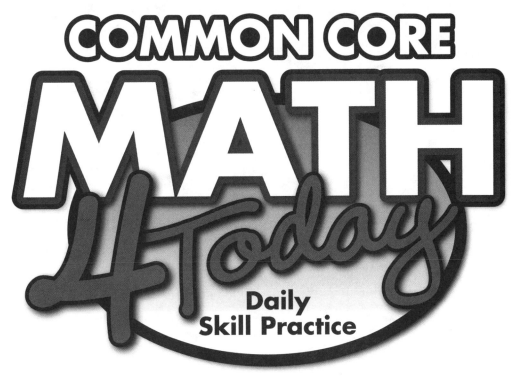

**Daily
Skill Practice**

Grade K

Erin McCarthy

Carson-Dellosa Publishing, LLC
Greensboro, North Carolina

Credits

Content Editors: Jennifer B. Stith and Elise Craver
Copy Editor: Sandra Ogle

Visit *carsondellosa.com* for correlations to Common Core, state, national, and Canadian provincial standards.

Carson-Dellosa Publishing, LLC
PO Box 35665
Greensboro, NC 27425 USA
carsondellosa.com

ISBN 978-1-62442-598-1
04-214161151

Table of Contents

Common Core Math 4 Today: Daily Skill Practice is a perfect supplement to any classroom math curriculum. Students' math skills will grow as they work on numbers, operations, algebraic thinking, place value, measurement, data, and geometry.

This book covers 40 weeks of daily practice. Four math problems a week will provide students with ample practice in math skills. A separate assessment of five questions is included for the fifth day of each week.

Various skills and concepts are reinforced throughout the book through activities that align to the Common Core State Standards. To view these standards, please see the Common Core State Standards Alignment Matrix on pages 7 and 8.

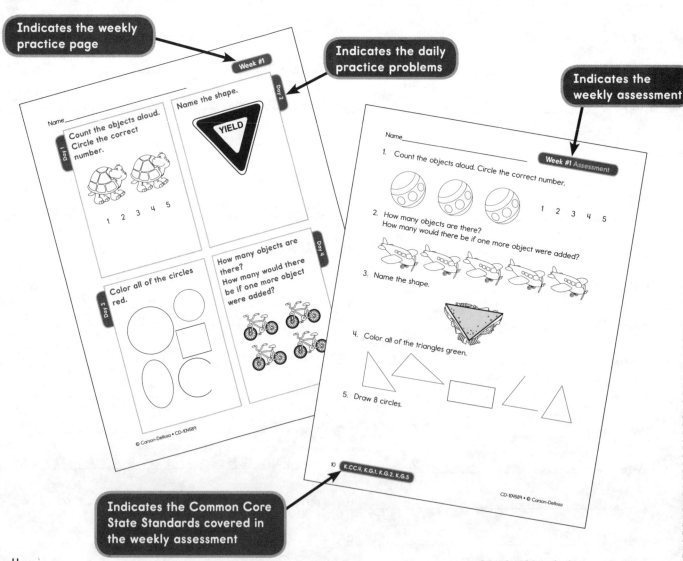

Indicates the weekly practice page

Indicates the daily practice problems

Indicates the weekly assessment

Indicates the Common Core State Standards covered in the weekly assessment

Incorporating the Standards for Mathematical Practice

The daily practice problems and weekly assessments in *Common Core Math 4 Today: Daily Skill Practice* help students achieve proficiency with the grade-level Common Core State Standards. Throughout the year, students should also work on building their comfort with the Standards for Mathematical Practice. Use the following suggestions to extend the problems in *Common Core Math 4 Today: Daily Skill Practice*.

1. **Make sense of problems and persevere in solving them.**

   Students should make sure that they understand a problem before trying to solve it. After solving, students should check their answers, often just by asking themselves if their answers make sense in the context of the question. Incorporate the following ideas into your Math 4 Today time:

   - Encourage students to underline the important parts of word problems and to draw lines through any extra information.
   - Allow students to talk through their answers with partners and explain why they think their answers make sense.

2. **Reason abstractly and quantitatively.**

   Students should be able to represent problems with numbers and symbols without losing the original meaning of the numbers and the symbols. A student who is successful at this practice will be able to reason about questions related to the original problem and use flexibility in solving problems. Incorporate the following ideas into your Math 4 Today time:

   - Ask students questions to extend the problems. For example, if a problem asks students to evenly divide a set of 10, ask them to describe what they would do if the set increased to 11.
   - Have students choose a computation problem and write a word problem to accompany it.

3. **Construct viable arguments and critique the reasoning of others.**

   Students should understand mathematical concepts well enough to be able to reason about and prove or disprove answers. As students become more comfortable with mathematical language, they should use math talk to explain their thinking. Incorporate the following ideas into your Math 4 Today time:

   - Have students work with partners and use mathematical language to explain their ways of thinking about a problem.
   - Encourage students to use manipulatives and drawings to support their reasoning.

4. **Model with mathematics.**

   Students should apply their mathematical knowledge to situations in the real world. They can use drawings, graphs, charts, and other tools to make sense of situations, as well as use skills such as estimation to approach a problem before solving it. Incorporate the following ideas into your Math 4 Today time:

- Encourage students to take a problem they have solved and explain how it could help them solve a problem in their own lives.
- Ask students to identify tools, such as charts or graphs, that could help them solve a problem.

5. **Use appropriate tools strategically.**

   Students should be able to use a range of tools to help them solve problems, as well as make decisions about which tools to use in different situations. Proficient students will use skills such as estimation to evaluate if the tools helped them solve the problem correctly. Incorporate the following ideas into your Math 4 Today time:

   - Ask students to discuss which tools would be most and least helpful in solving a problem.
   - As a class, discuss how two students using the same tool could have arrived at the same answer. Encourage students to identify the errors and the limitations in using certain tools.

6. **Attend to precision.**

   Students should be thorough in their use of mathematical symbols and labels. They should understand that without them, and without understanding their meanings, math problems are not as meaningful. Incorporate the following ideas into your Math 4 Today time:

   - Ask students to explain how a problem or an answer would change if a label on a graph were changed.
   - Have students go on a scavenger hunt for the week to identify units of measure in the problems, operations symbols, or graph labels.

7. **Look for and make use of structure.**

   Students identify and use patterns to help them extend their knowledge to new concepts. Understanding patterns and structure will also help students be flexible in their approaches to solving problems. Incorporate the following ideas into your Math 4 Today time:

   - Have students become pattern detectives and look for any patterns in each week's problems.
   - Ask students to substitute a different set of numbers into a problem and see if any patterns emerge.

8. **Look for and express regularity in repeated reasoning.**

   Students are able to use any patterns they notice to find shortcuts that help them solve other problems. They can observe a problem with an eye toward finding repetition, instead of straight computation. Incorporate the following ideas into your Math 4 Today time:

   - Allow students to share any shortcuts they may find during their problem solving. As a class, try to understand why the shortcuts work.
   - When students find patterns, have them explain how the patterns could help them solve other problems.

CD-104589 • © Carson-Dellosa

STANDARD	W1	W2	W3	W4	W5	W6	W7	W8	W9	W10	W11	W12	W13	W14	W15	W16	W17	W18	W19	W20
K.CC.3						●	●	●	●	●	●	●	●	●	●	●	●	●	●	●
K.CC.4a	●	●	●	●	●	●	●	●	●	●	●	●	●	●	●	●	●	●	●	●
K.CC.4b	●	●	●	●	●	●	●	●	●	●	●	●	●	●	●	●	●	●	●	●
K.CC.4c	●	●	●	●	●	●	●	●	●	●						●			●	●
K.CC.5	●	●	●	●	●	●	●	●	●	●	●		●	●	●	●	●	●	●	●
K.CC.6											●	●	●	●	●	●	●	●	●	●
K.CC.7																				
K.OA.1																				
K.OA.2																				
K.OA.3																				
K.OA.4																				
K.OA.5																				
K.NBT.1											●	●	●	●	●	●	●	●	●	●
K.MD.1											●		●		●		●		●	
K.MD.2																				
K.MD.3																				
K.G.1	●	●	●	●	●	●	●	●	●	●								●		●
K.G.2	●	●	●	●	●	●	●	●	●	●		●		●		●				
K.G.3																				
K.G.4																				
K.G.5	●	●	●	●	●	●	●	●	●	●										
K.G.6																				

W = Week

Because of the verbal nature of standards K.CC.1 and K.CC.2, they are not included in this book. Various activities may be adapted to address them.

Common Core State Standards Alignment Matrix

STANDARD	W21	W22	W23	W24	W25	W26	W27	W28	W29	W30	W31	W32	W33	W34	W35	W36	W37	W38	W39	W40
K.CC.3	●	●	●	●	●									●			●		●	
K.CC.4a	●	●	●	●										●			●			
K.CC.4b	●	●	●	●										●			●			
K.CC.4c																				
K.CC.5		●		●										●			●		●	
K.CC.6														●			●			●
K.CC.7	●		●		●		●	●	●		●		●		●		●		●	
K.OA.1	●		●		●		●		●		●		●		●		●	●	●	
K.OA.2	●				●		●		●	●								●		●
K.OA.3	●		●		●		●		●		●					●	●			
K.OA.4		●		●		●		●		●		●				●	●			
K.OA.5	●		●		●	●		●	●							●			●	●
K.NBT.1												●			●					●
K.MD.1												●								
K.MD.2		●		●		●		●		●		●				●				
K.MD.3		●		●	●															
K.G.1																				
K.G.2													●					●		
K.G.3		●		●		●		●		●			●							
K.G.4																●				
K.G.5																●		●		
K.G.6											●		●		●					

W = Week

Because of the verbal nature of standards K.CC.1 and K.CC.2, they are not included in this book. Various activities may be adapted to address them.

CD-104589 • © Carson-Dellosa

Day 1

Count the objects aloud. Circle the correct number.

1   2   3   4   5

Day 2

Name the shape.

Day 3

Color all of the circles red.

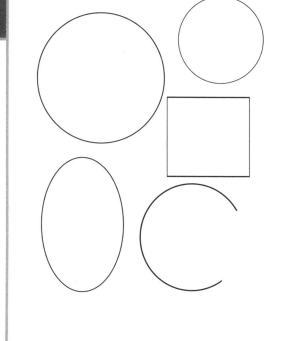

Day 4

How many objects are there?
How many would there be if one more object were added?

Name_____

1. Count the objects aloud. Circle the correct number.

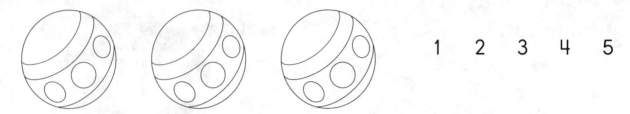

                                  1   2   3   4   5

2. How many objects are there?
   How many would there be if one more object were added?

3. Name the shape.

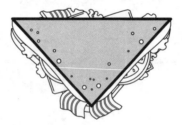

4. Color all of the triangles green.

5. Draw 8 circles.

 K.CC.4, K.G.1, K.G.2, K.G.5　　　　　　　　　CD-104589 • © Carson-Dellosa

Day 1

Name the shape.

Day 2

Count the objects aloud. Circle the correct number.

1   2   3   4   5

Day 3

How many objects are there?
How many would there be if one more object were added?

Day 4

Color all of the squares blue.

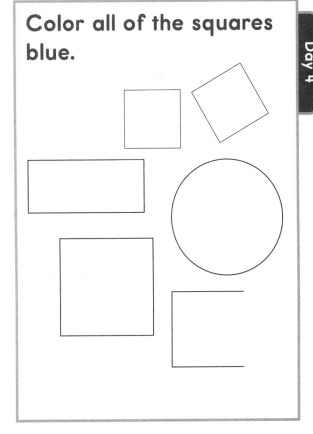

Name_____

1. Draw 4 rectangles.

2. Count the objects aloud. Circle the correct number.

       1   2   3   4   5   6   7

3. How many objects are there?
    How many would there be if one more object were added?

4. Name the shape.

    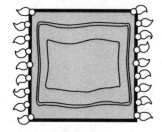

5. Color all of the circles red.

    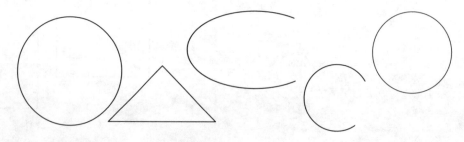

    CD-104589 • © Carson-Dellosa

Name_____

Day 1

Color all of the triangles green.

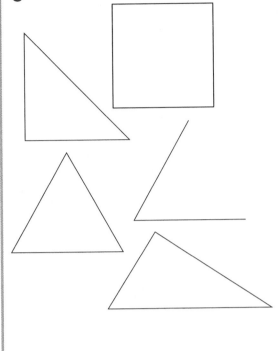

Day 2

How many objects are there?
How many would there be if one more object were added?

Day 3

Count the objects aloud. Circle the correct number.

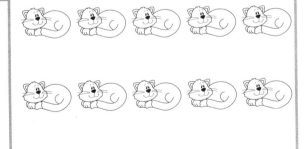

8   9   10   11   12

Day 4

Name the shape.

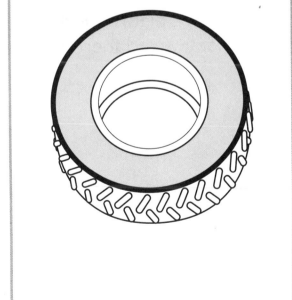

13

1. Color all of the hexagons purple.

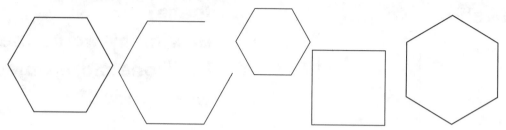

2. Draw 5 squares.

3. Count the objects aloud. Circle the correct number.

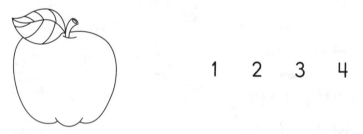

1   2   3   4   5

4. How many objects are there?
   How many would there be if one more object were added?

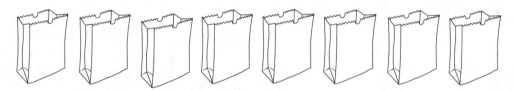

5. Name the shape.

K.CC.4, K.G.1, K.G.2, K.G5

Name_____

Day 1

How many objects are there?
How many would there be if one more object were added?

Day 2

Name the shape.

Day 3

Color all of the cubes pink.

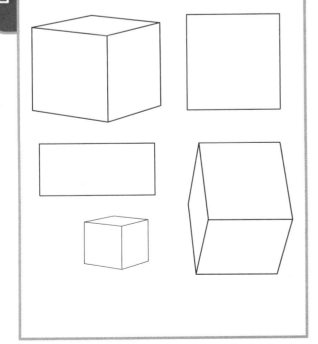

Day 4

Count the objects aloud. Circle the correct number.

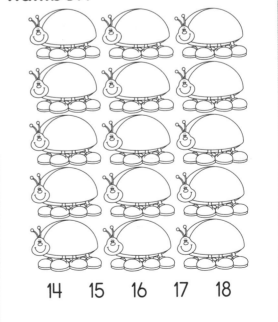

14   15   16   17   18

15

Name_____

1. Name the shape.

2. Color all of the squares blue.

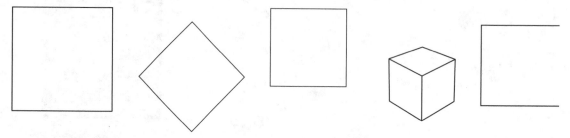

3. Draw 6 triangles.

4. Count the objects aloud. Circle the correct number.

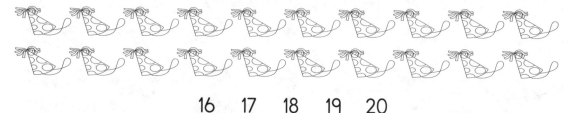

16   17   18   19   20

5. How many objects are there?
   How many would there be if one more object were added?

K.CC.4, K.G.1, K.G.2, K.G.5   CD-104589 • © Carson-Dellosa

Name_____

Day 1

Count the objects aloud. Circle the correct number.

12   13   14   15   16

Day 2

Name the shape.

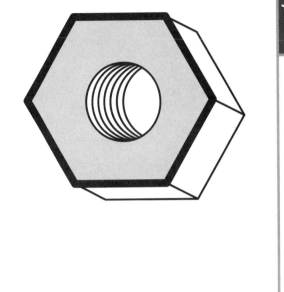

Day 3

Color all of the hexagons purple.

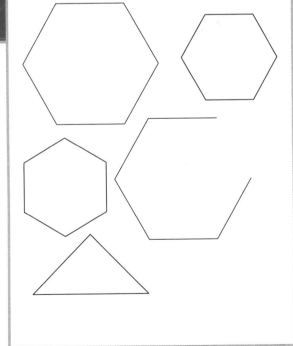

Day 4

How many objects are there?
How many would there be if one more object were added?

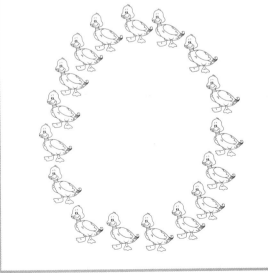

Name_____

1. How many objects are there?
   How many would there be if one more object were added?

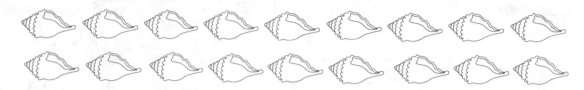

2. Name the shape.

3. Color all of the cylinders yellow.

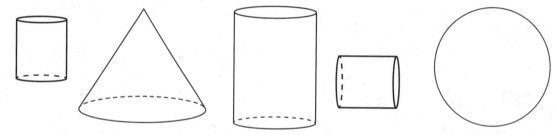

4. Draw 12 circles.

5. Count the objects aloud. Circle the correct number.

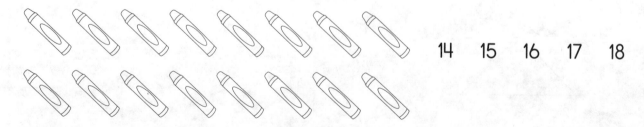

14   15   16   17   18

K.CC.4, K.G.1, K.G.2, K.G.5   CD-104589 • © Carson-Dellosa

Day 1

Color all of the cones brown.

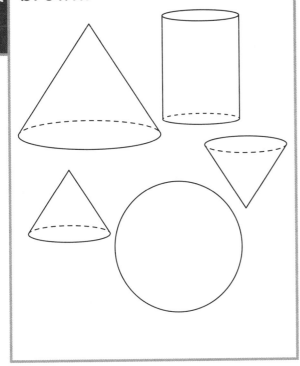

Day 2

Count the objects aloud. Write the correct number. _____

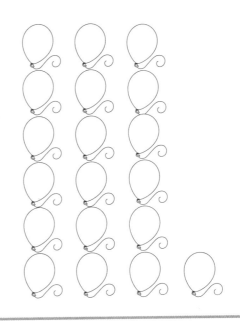

Day 3

How many objects are there?
How many would there be if one more object were added?

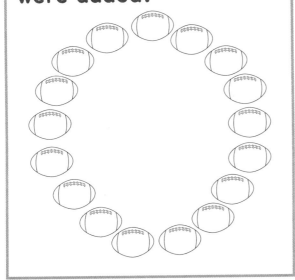

Day 4

Name the shapes.
Tell where the die is compared to the sign.

YIELD

1. Count the objects aloud. Write the correct number. _____

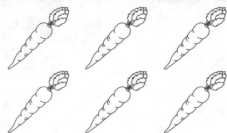

2. How many objects are there?
   How many would there be if one more object were added?

3. Name the shapes. Tell where the cake is compared to the sandwich.

 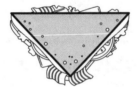

4. Color all of the cubes green.

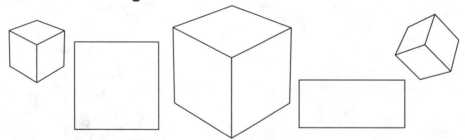

5. Draw 15 rectangles.

K.CC.3, K.CC.4, K.G.1, K.G.2, K.G.5 CD-104589 • © Carson-Dellosa

Name_____

Name the shapes.
Tell where the can is
compared to the map.

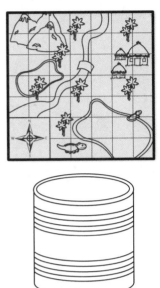

How many objects are
there?
How many would there
be if one more object
were added?

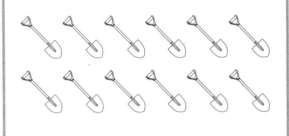

Count the objects
aloud. Write the correct
number. _____

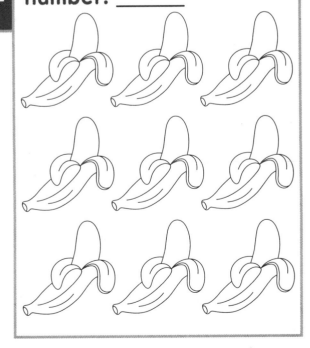

Color all of the cylinders
yellow.

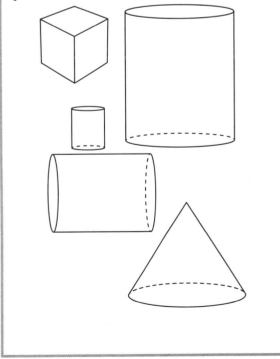

1. Draw 18 triangles.

2. Count the objects aloud. Write the correct number. _____

3. How many objects are there?
   How many would there be if one more object were added?

4. Name the shapes. Tell where the rug is compared to the soft drink can.

5. Color all of the rectangles orange.

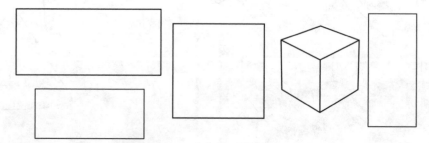

K.CC.3, K.CC.4, K.G.1, K.G.2, K.G.5

Day 1

How many objects are there?
How many would there be if one more object were added?

Day 2

Color all of the rectangles orange.

Day 3

Name the shapes.
Tell where the tire is compared to the ice-cream cone.

Day 4

Count the objects aloud. Write the correct number. _____

1. Color all of the spheres brown.

2. Draw 20 squares.

3. Count the objects aloud. Write the correct number. _____

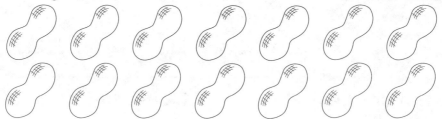

4. How many objects are there?
   How many would there be if one more object were added?

5. Name the shapes. Tell where the ring is compared to the traffic cone.

Name_____

Day 1

Count the objects aloud. Write the correct number. _____

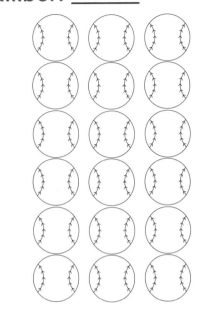

Day 2

Name the shapes. Tell where the ball is compared to the window.

Day 3

Color the spheres orange.

Day 4

How many objects are there?
How many would there be if one more object were added?

1. How many objects are there?
   How many would there be if one more object were added?

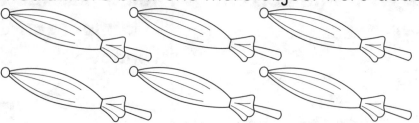

2. Name the shapes. Tell where the door is compared to Earth.

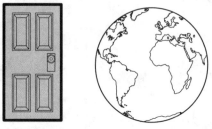

3. Color all of the cones brown.

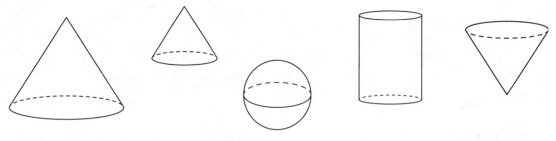

4. Draw 7 hexagons.

5. Count the objects aloud. Write the correct number. _____

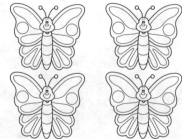

K.CC.3, K.CC.4, K.G.1, K.G.2, K.G.5

CD-104589 • © Carson-Dellosa

Name_____

Day 1

Color all of the cubes blue.

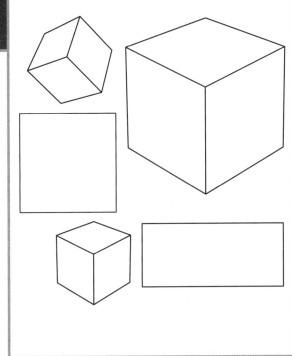

Day 2

Count the objects aloud. Write the correct number. _____

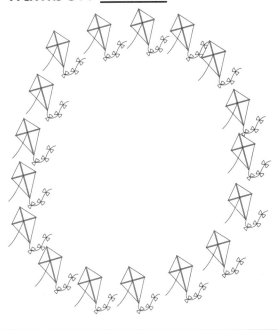

Day 3

How many objects are there?
How many would there be if one more object were added?

Day 4

Name the shapes. Tell where the cereal is compared to the nut.

1.   Count the objects aloud. Write the correct number. _____

2.   How many objects are there?
      How many would there be if one more object were added?

3.   Name the shapes. Tell where the box is compared to the remote control.

4.   Color all of the rectangles orange.

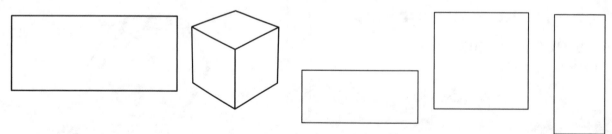

5.   Draw 16 circles.

Day 1

Circle the set that has more objects.

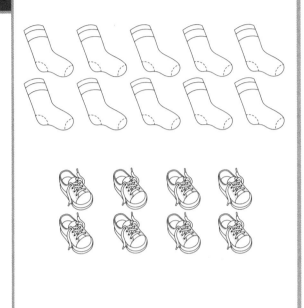

Day 2

Use the ten frame to show the number sentence.

10 and 2 is 12.

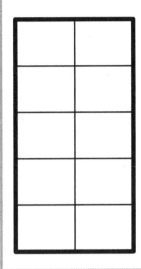

Day 3

Circle the word that best describes the feather.

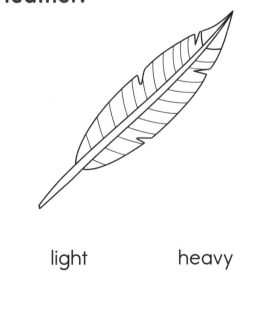

light   heavy

Day 4

Count the objects aloud. Write the correct number. _____

Name_____

1. Circle the set that has more objects.

 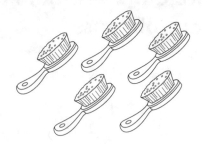

2. Use the ten frame to show the number sentence.

10 and 5 is 15.

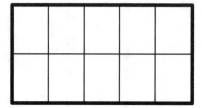

3. Circle the word that best describes the car.

light   heavy

4. Count the objects aloud. Write the correct number. _____

5. Circle the set that has more objects.

Day 1

Draw a line to connect each shape with its name.

square

circle

triangle

Day 2

Circle the set that has more objects.

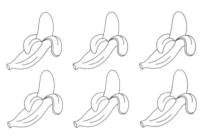

Day 3

Use the ten frame to show the number sentence.

10 and 3 is 13.

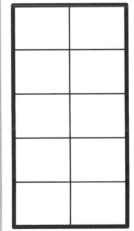

Day 4

Count the objects aloud. Write the correct number. _____

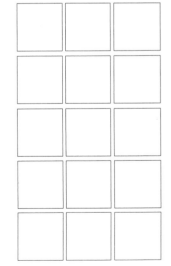

1. Use the ten frame to show the number sentence.

    10 and 8 is 18.
    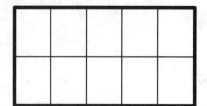

2. Circle the set that has more objects.

     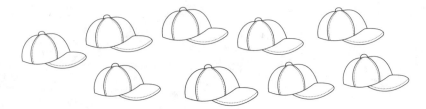

3. Use the ten frame to show the number sentence.

    10 and 7 is 17.
    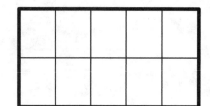

4. Count the objects aloud. Write the correct number. _____

5. Draw a line to connect each shape with its name.

    rectangle

    hexagon

    square

Day 1

Circle the word that best describes a baby.

tall   short

Day 2

Count the objects aloud. Write the correct number. _____

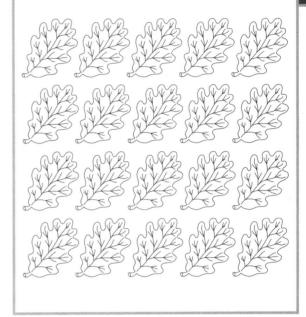

Day 3

Circle the set that has more objects.

Day 4

Use the ten frame to show the number sentence.

10 and 4 is 14.

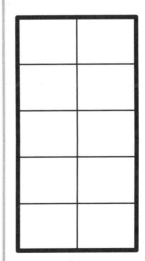

Name_____

1. Count the objects aloud. Write the correct number. _____

2. Circle the set that has more objects.

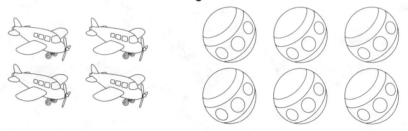

3. Circle the set that has more objects.

4. Use the ten frame to show the number sentence.

10 and 9 is 19.
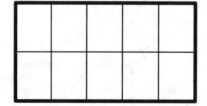

5. Circle the word that best describes the tree.

tall   short

Day 1

Use the ten frame to show the number sentence.

10 and 6 is 16.

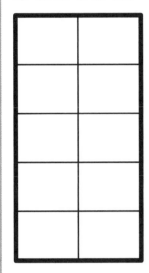

Day 2

Count the objects aloud. Write the correct number. _____

Day 3

Draw a line to connect each shape with its name.

     cube

     cylinder

   cone

Day 4

Circle the set that has more objects.

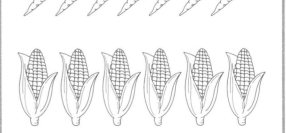

1. Count the objects aloud. Write the correct number. _____

2. Draw a line to connect each shape with its name.

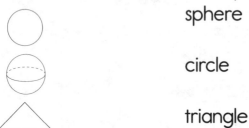

                    sphere

                    circle

                    triangle

3. Use the ten frame to show the number sentence.

10 and 4 is 14.

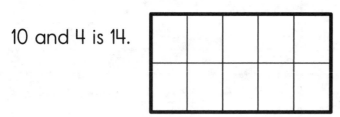

4. Circle the set that has more objects.

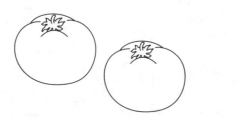

5. Use the ten frame to show the number sentence.

10 and 8 is 18.

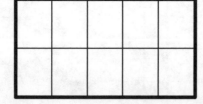

Name_____

Day 1

Circle the set that has more objects.

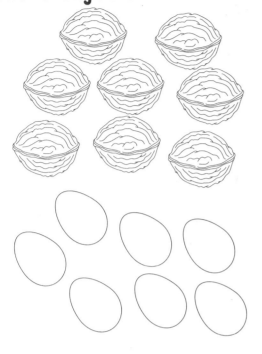

Day 2

Use the ten frame to show the number sentence.

10 and 1 is 11.

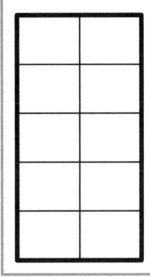

Day 3

Circle the word that best describes the teddy bear.

light   heavy

Day 4

Count the objects aloud. Write the correct number. _____

Name_____

1. Use the ten frame to show the number sentence.

   10 and 6 is 16.
   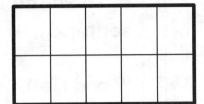

2. Circle the word that best describes the bear.

   light   heavy

3. Count the objects aloud. Write the correct number. _____

4. Circle the set that has more objects.

5. Circle the set that has more objects.

 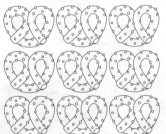

K.CC.3, K.CC.4, K.CC.5, K.CC.6, K.NBT.1, K.MD.1

Name_____

Day 1

Write the number of objects. _____
Write the number of objects there would be if one more object were added. _____

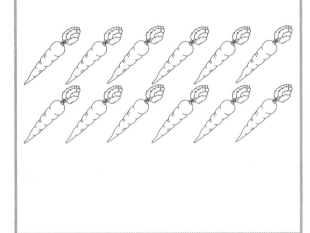

Day 2

Circle the set that has less objects.

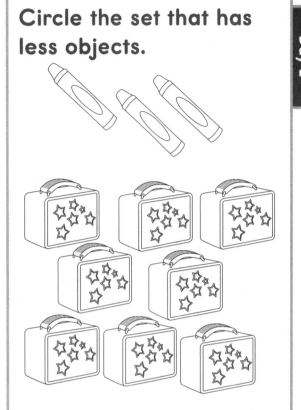

Day 3

Write the number sentence.

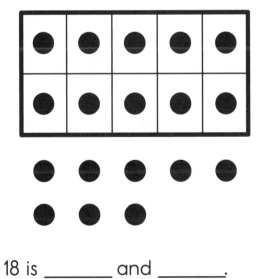

18 is _____ and _____.

Day 4

Draw a line to connect each shape with its name.

hexagon

sphere

rectangle

1. Circle the set that has less objects.

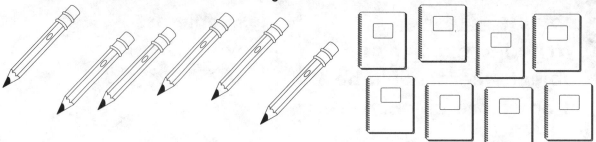

2. Write the number sentence.

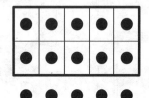

15 is _____ and _____.

3. Write the number of objects. _____ Write the number of objects there would be if one more object were added. _____

4. Draw a line to connect each shape with its name.

           cube

           cylinder

           cone

5. Write the number sentence.

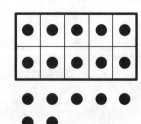

17 is _____ and _____.

K.CC.3, K.CC.4, K.CC.6, K.NBT.1, K.G.2

Name_____

Day 1

Circle the word that best describes the girl's hair.

long   short

Day 2

Count the objects aloud. Write the correct number. _____

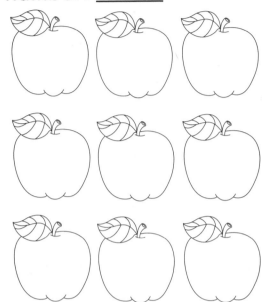

Day 3

Circle the set that has less objects.

Day 4

Write the number sentence.

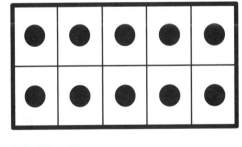

13 is _____ and _____.

41

1. Circle the set that has less objects.

2. Circle the set that has less objects.

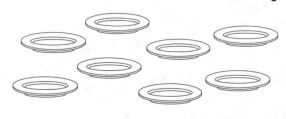 

3. Write the number sentence.

14 is _____ and _____.

4. Circle the word that best describes the boy's hair.

long   short

5. Count the objects aloud. Write the correct number. _____

K.CC.3, K.CC.4, K.CC.5, K.CC.6, K.NBT.1, K.MD.1   CD-104589 • © Carson-Dellosa

Name_____

Day 1

Write the number sentence.

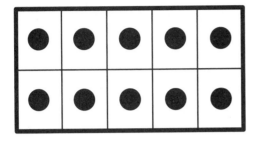

12 is _____ and _____.

Day 2

Count the objects aloud. Write the correct number. _____

Day 3

Color all of the objects that are the same shape as △.

Day 4

Circle the set that has less objects.

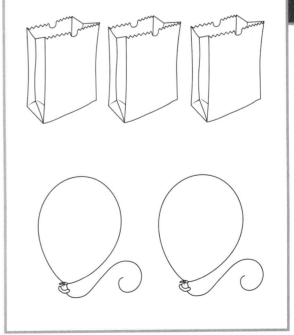

1. Color all of the objects that are the same shape as .

  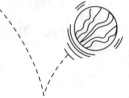  

2. Write the number sentence.

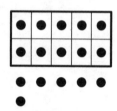

16 is _____ and _____.

3. Circle the set that has less objects.

 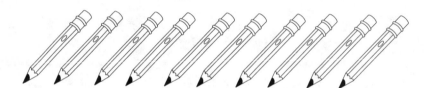

4. Write the number sentence.

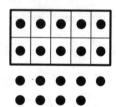

19 is _____ and _____.

5. Count the objects aloud. Write the correct number. _____

K.CC.3, K.CC.4, K.CC.5, K.CC.6, K.NBT.1, K.G.1

Day 1

Draw lines to match the sets that have the same number of objects.

Day 2

Write the number sentence.

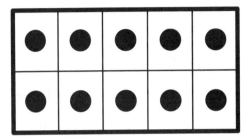

11 is _____ and _____.

Day 3

Circle the word that best describes the toy truck.

light   heavy

Day 4

Write the number of objects. _____
Write the number of objects there would be if one more object were added. _____

1. Circle the word that best describes the truck.

light   heavy

2. Write the number of objects. _____ Write the number of objects there would be if one more object were added. _____

3. Draw lines to match the sets that have the same number of objects.

4. Draw lines to match the sets that have the same number of objects.

5. Write the number sentence.

17 is _____ and _____.

K.CC.3, K.CC.4, K.CC.5, K.CC.6, K.NBT.1, K.MD.1

Name_____

Write the number of objects. _____
Write the number of objects there would be if one more object were added. _____

Draw lines to match the sets that have the same number of objects.

Write the number sentence.

16 is _____ and _____.

Color all of the objects that are the same shape as .

1. Write the number sentence.

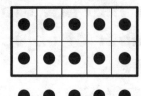

15 is _____ and _____.

2. Write the number of objects. _____ Write the number of objects there would be if one more object were added. _____

3. Color all of the objects that are the same shape as .

   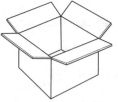

4. Write the number sentence.

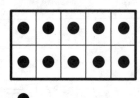

11 is _____ and _____.

5. Draw lines to match the sets that have the same number of objects.

K.CC.3, K.CC.4, K.CC.5, K.CC.6, K.NBT.1, K.G.1

Day 1

Circle the number that is greater.

5   3

Day 2

Count each set of rabbits. Write the number under each set. Write the sum at the end of the number sentence.

_____ + _____ = _____

Day 3

Daniel picked 5 pumpkins. Sam picked 3 pumpkins. Write a number sentence to show how many pumpkins the boys picked altogether.

_____ + _____ = _____

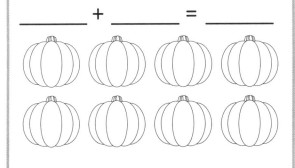

Day 4

Brad has 6 pieces of fruit in his bag. Draw a picture of all of the ways you can show the bananas and oranges in his bag.

Name_____

1. Circle the number that is greater.

   4   6

2. Count each set of birds. Write the number under each set. Write the sum at the end of the number sentence.

   _____ + _____ = _____

3. Kade blew up 4 balloons for the harvest party. Lisa blew up 2 balloons. Write a number sentence to show how many balloons the girls blew up altogether.

   _____ + _____ = _____

4. Paul has 5 toy vehicles in a box. Draw a picture of all of the ways you can show the trucks and cars in his box.

5. Circle the number that is greater.

   9   8

Name_____

Nicole needs 10 apples to make an apple pie. If she has only 3 apples, how many more apples does she need? Draw a picture to show your thinking.

Circle the larger object.

Count the number of each animal. Answer each question.

How many 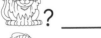? _____

How many ? _____

How many ? _____

How many 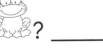? _____

Color the flat shape.

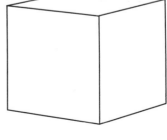

1.   Amanda needs 10 more red beads to finish making her necklace. If she has only 4 red beads, how many more red beads does she need? Draw a picture to show your thinking.

2. Circle the larger object.

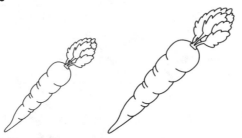

3.   Count the number of each weather picture. Answer each question.

How many ? _____

How many ? _____

How many ? _____

How many ? _____

4.   Color the flat shape.

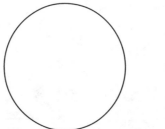
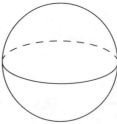

5.   Cole needs 10 more seashells to finish making his craft project. If he has only 2 seashells, how many more seashells does he need? Draw a picture to show your thinking.

 K.CC.5, K.OA.4, K.MD.2, K.MD.3, K.G.3   CD-104589 • © Carson-Dellosa

Name_____

Day 1

Count each set of snakes. Write the number under each set. Write the sum at the end of the number sentence.

_____ + _____ = _____

Day 2

Jay and his brother helped their dad decorate tables for the party. Jay decorated 2 tables, and his brother decorated 8 tables. Draw a picture to show how many tables the boys decorated altogether.

Day 3

Hector has 7 players on his baseball team. Some are boys, and some are girls. Draw a picture of all of the ways you can show the players on Hector's team.

Day 4

Circle the number that is greater.

7   2

1. Draw 2 more buttons. Write the number sentence.

_____ + _____ = _____

2. Dez has 4 teddy bears. Some are brown, and some are white. Draw a picture of all of the ways you can show the teddy bears that Dez has.

3. Three monkeys are resting in a tree. Four alligators are under the tree. Draw a picture to show how many animals are in and under the tree.

4. Count each set of fish. Write the number under each set. Write the sum at the end of the number sentence.

_____ + _____ = _____

5. Circle the number that is greater.

5   6

Day 1

Circle the larger object.

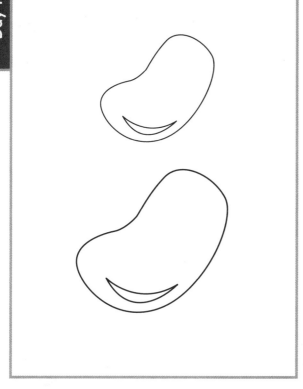

Day 2

Count the number of each shape. Answer each question.

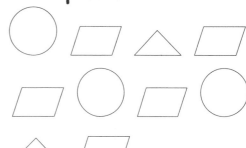

How many △? _____

How many ▱? _____

How many ◯? _____

Day 3

Color the solid shape.

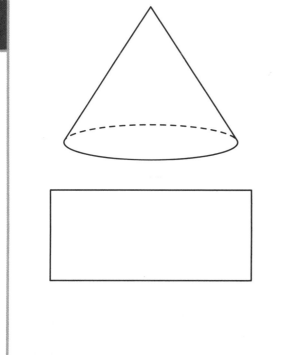

Day 4

Chang needs 10 players to make a basketball team. If he has only 5 players, how many more players does he need? Draw a picture to show your thinking.

Name_____

1. Circle the larger object.

2. Color the solid shape.

3. Count the number of each toy. Answer each question.

How many ? _____
How many ? _____
How many ? _____
How many ? _____

4. Circle the larger object.

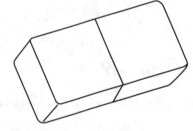 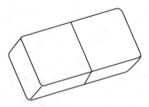

5. Ellen needs 10 flowers to fill her flower basket. If she has only 7 flowers, how many more flowers does she need? Draw a picture to show your thinking.

Day 1

Cindy has 8 pets at home. Some of them are cats, and some of them are dogs. Draw a picture of all of the ways you can show the pets at Cindy's house.

Day 2

Circle the number that is greater.

7   3

Day 3

Count the dots on each domino. Solve each problem.

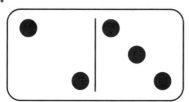

2 + 3 = _____

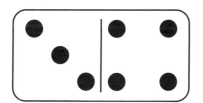

3 + 4 = _____

Day 4

Jose saw 5 frogs. Abigail saw 2 frogs. Write a number sentence to show how many frogs Jose and Abigail saw in all.

_____ + _____ = _____

1. Count the dots on each domino. Solve each problem.

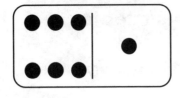 

   6 + 1 = _____   7 + 3 = _____

2. Circle the number that is greater.

           2   8

3. Count the dots on each domino. Solve each problem.

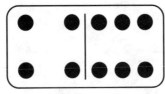 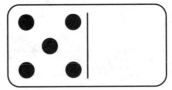

   4 + 6 = _____   5 + 0 = _____

4. A leopard was lying in a tree. He saw 3 monkeys swinging from tree to tree. Write a number sentence to show how many animals were in the trees.

    _____ + _____ = _____

5. Brian has 3 books in his desk. Some of them are fiction, and some of them are nonfiction. Draw a picture of all of the ways you can show the books in Brian's desk.

 K.CC.7, K.OA.1, K.OA.2, K.OA.3   CD-104589 • © Carson-Dellosa

Name_____

Day 1

Ask each of 8 friends which playground object is his or her favorite. Draw a tally mark to show each friend's vote.

 _____

 _____

 _____

Day 2

Circle the shorter object.

Day 3

Ella needs 10 buttons to sew on her sweater. If she has only 6 buttons, how many more buttons does she need? Draw a picture to show your thinking.

Day 4

Color the flat shape.

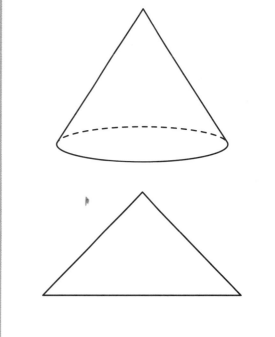

1. Color the solid shape.

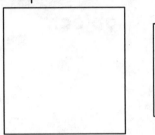 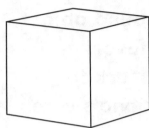

2. Dave needs 10 lollipops to share with 10 friends. If he has only 2 lollipops, how many more lollipops does he need? Draw a picture to show your thinking.

3. Circle the shorter object.

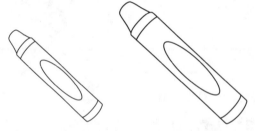

4. Ask each of 8 friends which pet is his or her favorite. Draw a tally mark to show each friend's vote.

 _____    _____

 _____   _____

5. Color the flat shape.

 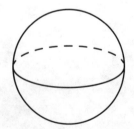

K.OA.4, K.MD.2, K.MD.3, K.G.3

Day 1

Pablo hit 7 baseballs. Two of them were home runs and went outside the park. Act out the problem to show how many baseballs Pablo hit inside the park.

Day 2

Write a number sentence that matches the picture.

_____ – _____ = _____

Day 3

Circle the number that is greater.

7   4

Day 4

Greg has 2 different pieces of candy in his pocket. Draw a picture of all of the ways you can show the different candy in Greg's pocket.

Name_____

1. Grace has 9 games on a shelf. Some of them are card games, and some of them are dice games. Draw a picture of all of the ways you can show the games on Grace's shelf.

2. Molly's team had 7 baseball gloves. They shared 3 of those with the other team. Act out the problem to show how many baseball gloves Molly's team has left.

3. Circle the number that is greater.

   9   6

4. Write a number sentence that matches the picture.

   _____ – _____ = _____

5. Eight players are on one team. Four of the players are in the dugout. The rest are on the field. Act out the problem to show how many players are on the field.

Day 1

Circle the number that is less.

9   6

Day 2

Jan needs 10 forks to set the table. If she has only 8 forks, how many more forks does she need? Draw a picture to show your thinking.

Day 3

Circle the longer object.

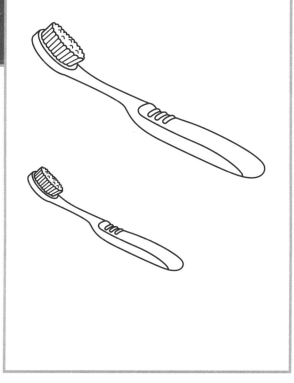

Day 4

Color the solid shape.

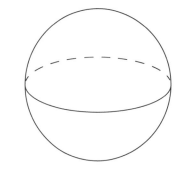

Name_____

1. Color the solid shape.

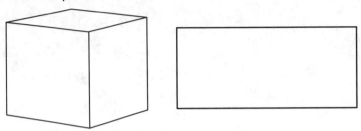

2. Circle the number that is less.

        4   2

3. Quan needs 10 canned goods to bring in for his class food drive. If he has only 9 canned goods, how many more canned goods does he need? Draw a picture to show your thinking.

4. Circle the longer object.

5. Circle the number that is less.

        1   5

 K.CC.7, K.OA.4, K.MD.2, K.G.3   CD-104589 • © Carson-Dellosa

Day 1

Uma has 10 dresses hanging in her closet. Some of the dresses are short, and some of the dresses are long. Draw a picture of one of the ways you can show the dresses in Uma's closet.

Day 2

Nine fish were in the tank at the pet store. Bailey bought 5 of the fish. She took them home with her. Draw a picture to show how many fish are left at the pet store.

Day 3

Write a number sentence that matches the picture.

_____ – _____ = _____

Day 4

Circle the number that is less.

10   3

1. Circle the number that is less.

    7   5

2. Look at the picture. Write a number sentence that matches the picture.

   _____ - _____ = _____

3. Nine birds were sitting on the perch. Seven birds jumped down to eat some bird food. Draw a picture to show how many birds were left on the perch.

4. Victor has 4 cats in his home. Some of the cats are white, and some of the cats are gray. Draw a picture of one of the ways you can show the cats in Victor's home.

5. Write a number sentence that matches the picture.

   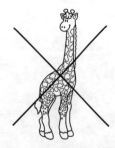   _____ - _____ = _____

Day 1

Color the flat shape.

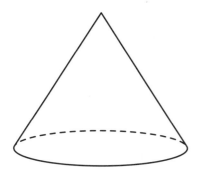

Day 2

Circle the taller ladder.

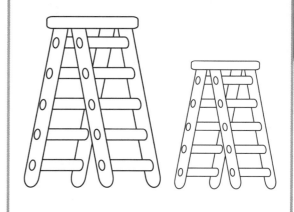

Day 3

Luke needs 10 hamburgers for his family picnic. If he has only 1 hamburger, how many more hamburgers does he need? Draw a picture to show your thinking.

Day 4

Lisa has 10 kittens. She gave 7 kittens away to her friends. Write a number sentence that matches the picture.

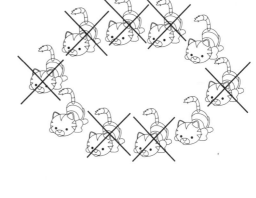

_____ - _____ = _____

1. Color the solid shape.

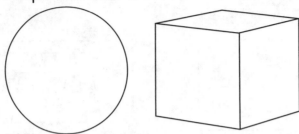

2. Rick had a bag of 9 strawberries. He shared 5 strawberries with Tara. Write a number sentence that matches the picture.

_____ - _____ = _____

3. Circle the longer object.

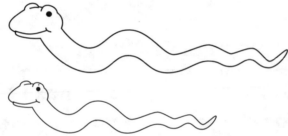

4. Pete needs 10 ice-cream cones for his birthday party. If he has only 5 ice-cream cones, how many more ice-cream cones does he need? Draw a picture to show your thinking.

5. Circle the taller person.

K.OA2, K.OA.4, K.MD.2, K.G.3

Day 1

Using pattern blocks, cover the hexagon with only red trapezoids. Trace the blocks you use onto the shape.

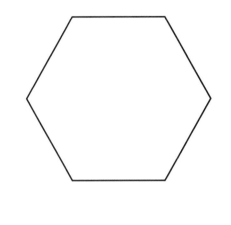

Day 2

Circle the number that is greater.

4   8

Day 3

Follow the directions. Write a number sentence to match.

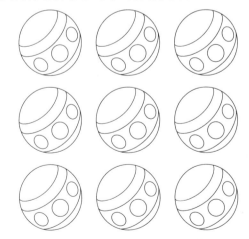

Color 6 yellow. Color 3 orange.

_____ + _____ = _____

Day 4

Complete the number sentences.

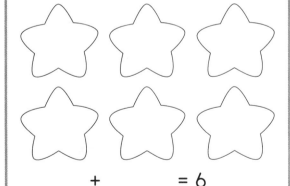

_____ + _____ = 6
_____ + _____ = 6
_____ + _____ = 6
_____ + _____ = 6
_____ + _____ = 6

1. Using pattern blocks, cover the hexagon with only blue parallelograms. Trace the blocks you use onto the shape.

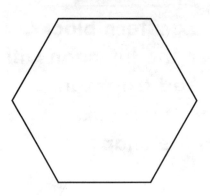

2. Circle the number that is greater.

9   7

3. Follow the directions. Write a number sentence to match.

Color 5 blue. Color 4 yellow.   _____ + _____ = _____

4. Complete the number sentences.

_____ + _____ = 9
_____ + _____ = 9
_____ + _____ = 9
_____ + _____ = 9
_____ + _____ = 9

5. Circle the number that is greater.

6   7

Day 1

Draw more umbrellas to make a set of 10.

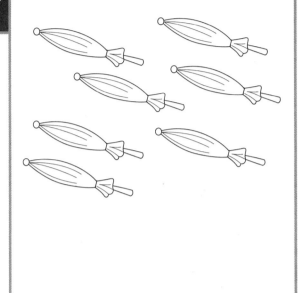

Day 2

Draw a picture to show the number 15.

Day 3

What are some ways you can measure a paper clip?

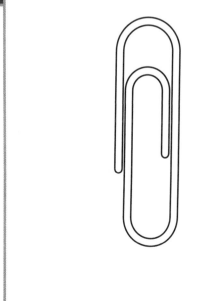

Day 4

Circle the object that weighs more.

Name_____

1. Draw more flowers to make a set of 10.

2. Draw a picture to show the number 13.

3. What are some ways you can measure a pencil?

4. Circle the object that weighs more.

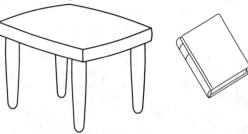

5. Draw a picture to show the number 16.

Name_____

Day 1

Circle the number that is less.

10   8

Day 2

Using pattern blocks, cover the hexagon with only green triangles. Trace the blocks you use onto the shape.

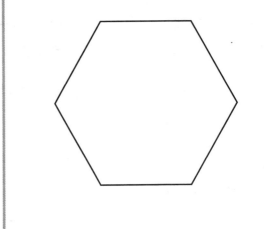

Day 3

Name the shape.

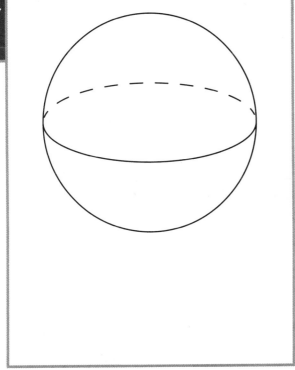

Day 4

Write a number sentence that matches the picture.

_____ − _____ = _____

1. Write a number sentence that matches the picture.

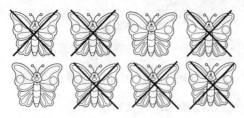

_____ – _____ = _____

2. Using pattern blocks, cover the trapezoid with only green triangles. Trace the blocks you use onto the shape.

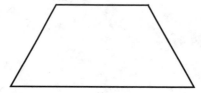

3. Name the shape.

4. Circle the number that is less.

6   9

5. Write a number sentence that matches the picture.

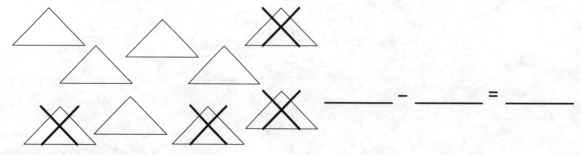

_____ – _____ = _____

K.CC.7, K.OA.1, K.G.2, K.G.6

Name_____

Day 1

Write the number of bananas. _____

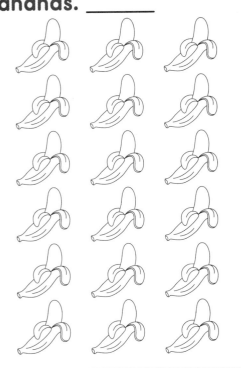

Day 2

Circle the set that has more objects.

Day 3

Color the solid shape.

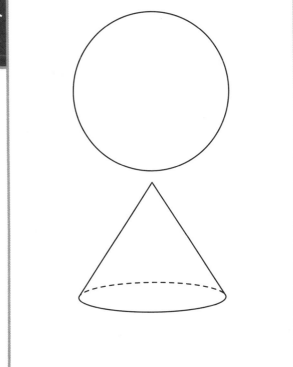

Day 4

Draw more apples to make a set of 10.

1. Draw more dots to make a set of 10.

2. Write the number of apples. _____

3. Draw more bananas to make a set of 10.

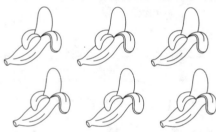

4. Circle the set that has more objects.

5. Color the solid shape.

 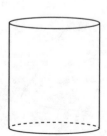

K.CC.3, K.CC.4, K.CC.5, K.CC.6, K.OA.4, K.G.3

Day 1

Draw a picture to show the number 17.

Day 2

Circle the number that is greater.

1   8

Day 3

Using pattern blocks, cover the trapezoid with one blue parallelogram and one green triangle. Trace the blocks you use onto the shape.

Day 4

Follow the directions. Write the number sentence.

Color 7 stars blue.
Color 0 stars orange.

_____ + _____ = _____

1. Draw a picture to show the number 19.

2. Follow the directions. Write the number sentence.

   Color 6 flowers pink.
   Color 4 flowers white.

   _____ + _____ = _____

3. Using pattern blocks, cover the hexagon with one green triangle, one blue parallelogram, and one red trapezoid. Trace the blocks you use onto the shape.

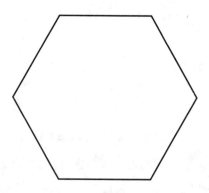

4. Circle the number that is greater.

   5   3

5. Follow the directions. Write the number sentence.

   Color 5 frogs blue.
   Color 3 frogs orange.

   _____ + _____ = _____

Name_____

Day 1

Circle the name of longer object.

pencil

ladder

Day 2

Describe how these two shapes are the same and how they are different.

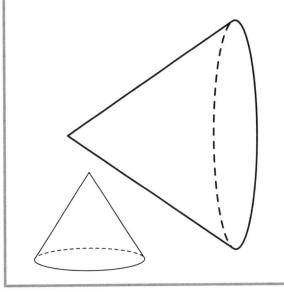

Day 3

Complete the number sentences.

_____ + _____ = 8

_____ + _____ = 8

_____ + _____ = 8

_____ + _____ = 8

_____ + _____ = 8

Day 4

Draw more circles to make a set of 10.

1. Circle the name of the longer object.

    a sheet of paper

    the classroom wall

2. Describe how these two shapes are the same and how they are different.

 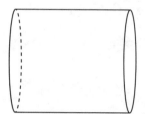

3. Complete the number sentences.

    _____ + _____ = 3

    _____ + _____ = 3

    _____ + _____ = 3

    _____ + _____ = 3

4. Draw more squares to make a set of 10.

5. Complete the number sentences.

    _____ + _____ = 10

    _____ + _____ = 10

    _____ + _____ = 10

    _____ + _____ = 10

K.OA.3, K.OA.4, K.MD.2, K.G.4, K.G.5

Day 1

Write the number of objects. _____

Day 2

Circle the set that has less objects.

Day 3

Circle the number that is less.

9   3

Day 4

Write a number sentence that matches the picture.

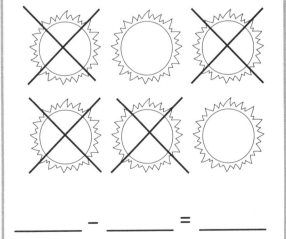

_____ – _____ = _____

1. Circle the set that has less objects.

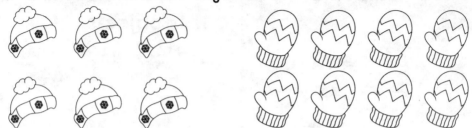

2. Write a number sentence that matches the picture.

_____ - _____ = _____

3. Circle the number that is less.

    7   1

4. Circle the set that has less objects.

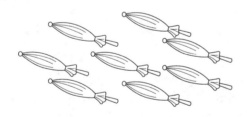   

5. Write the number of objects. _____

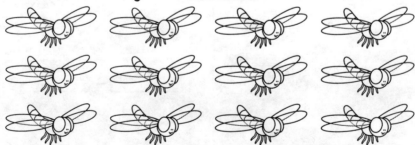

K.CC.3, K.CC.4, K.CC.5, K.CC.6, K.CC.7, K.OA.1, K.OA.5   CD-104589 • © Carson-Dellosa

Day 1

Amy saw 5 turtles in the pond. Bonnie saw 3 more turtles in the pond. Act out the problem to show how many turtles Amy and Bonnie saw in the pond.

Day 2

Complete the number sentences.

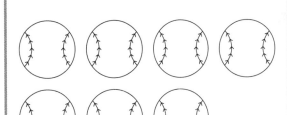

_____ + _____ = 7

_____ + _____ = 7

_____ + _____ = 7

_____ + _____ = 7

_____ + _____ = 7

Day 3

Draw more triangles to make a set of 10.

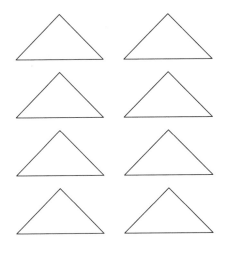

Day 4

Circle the name of the shape.

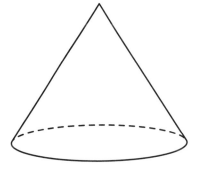

cone   cylinder

1. Circle the name of the shape.

square   cube

2. Count the set. Draw more hands to make a set of 10.

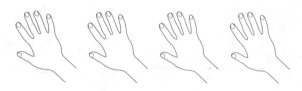

3. Ross bought 7 flowers for his teacher. Holly bought 2 flowers for her teacher. Act out the problem to show how many flowers Ross and Holly bought altogether.

4. Complete the number sentences.

_____ + _____ = 5

_____ + _____ = 5

_____ + _____ = 5

5. Draw more rectangles to make a set of 10.

K.OA.1, K.OA.2, K.OA.3, K.OA.4, K.G.2, K.G.5   CD-104589 • © Carson-Dellosa

Day 1

1 + 3 = _____

2 + 2 = _____

Day 2

Write the number of objects. _____

Day 3

Circle the number that is greater.

10   4

Day 4

Follow the directions. Write the number sentence.

Color 3 hearts red.
Color 5 hearts purple.

_____ + _____ = _____

Name_____

1. 3 + 1 = _____

    1 + 2 = _____

2. Write the number of objects. _____

3. Circle the number that is greater.

            8   9

4. Follow the directions. Write the number sentence.

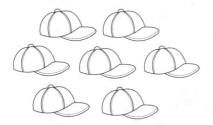   Color 6 hats green.
                        Color 1 hat red.

                        _____ + _____ = _____

5. Write the number of objects. _____

 K.CC.3, K.CC.5, K.CC.7, K.OA.1, K.OA.5   CD-104589 • © Carson-Dellosa

Day 1

Draw a picture to show the number 12.

Day 2

Zack and Jai hit the same amount of golf balls into the pond. If Zack hit 4 golf balls into the pond, how many golf balls did the boys hit into the pond altogether? Write a number sentence to solve the problem.

_____ + _____ = _____

Day 3

Circle the set that has less objects.

Day 4

5 – 3 = _____

2 – 1 = _____

1. Draw a picture to show the number 18.

2. 3 – 2 = _____

   1 – 1 = _____

3. Circle the set that has less objects.

4. 4 – 2 = _____

   5 – 5 = _____

5. Erin took 5 pictures on her vacation. Drew took 5 pictures on his vacation. Write a number sentence to show how many pictures Erin and Drew took altogether.

_____ + _____ = _____

K.CC.3, K.CC.6, K.OA.2, K.OA.5, K.NBT.1   CD-104589 • © Carson-Dellosa

Page 9
Day 1: 2; **Day 2:** triangle;
Day 3: Check students' answers;
Day 4: 4, 5

Page 10
1. 3; 2. 5, 6; 3. triangle; 4. Check students' answers; 5. Check students' answers.

Page 11
Day 1: square; **Day 2:** 5;
Day 3: 11, 12; **Day 4:** Check students' answers.

Page 12
1. Check students' answers; 2. 7; 3. 10, 11; 4. square; 5. Check students' answers.

Page 13
Day 1: Check students' answers;
Day 2: 12, 13; **Day 3:** 10;
Day 4: circle

Page 14
1. Check students' answers;
2. Check students' answers; 3. 1; 4. 8, 9; 5. circle

Page 15
Day 1: 13, 14; **Day 2:** rectangle;
Day 3: Check students' answers;
Day 4: 15

Page 16
1. rectangle; 2. Check students' answers; 3. Check students' answers; 4. 20; 5. 9, 10

Page 17
Day 1: 14; **Day 2:** hexagon;
Day 3: Check students' answers;
Day 4: 17, 18

Page 18
1. 18, 19; 2. cube; 3. Check students' answers; 4. Check students' answers; 5. 16

Page 19
Day 1: Check students' answers;
Day 2: 19; **Day 3:** 17, 18;
Day 4: cube, triangle; The die is above the sign.

Page 20
1. 6; 2. 13, 14; 3. cube, triangle; The cake is next to the sandwich; 4. Check students' answers; 5. Check students' answers.

Page 21
Day 1: square, cylinder; The can is below the map, or the map is above the can; **Day 2:** 12, 13; **Day 3:** 9; **Day 4:** Check students' answers.

Page 22
1. Check students' answers; 2. 8;
3. 12, 13; 4. square, cylinder; The soft drink can is next to the rug;
5. Check students' answers.

Page 23
Day 1: 19, 20; **Day 2:** Check students' answers; **Day 3:** cone, circle; The ice-cream cone is next to the tire; **Day 4:** 11

Page 24
1. Check students' answers;
2. Check students' answers; 3. 14;
4. 19, 20; 5. cone, circle; The ring is next to the traffic cone.

Page 25
Day 1: 18; **Day 2:** sphere, rectangle; The ball is next to the window; **Day 3:** Check students' answers; **Day 4:** 8, 9

Page 26
1. 6, 7; 2. rectangle, sphere; Earth is next to the door; 3. Check students' answers; 4. Check students' answers; 5. 4

Page 27
Day 1: Check students' answers; **Day 2:** 17; **Day 3:** 15, 16; **Day 4:** hexagon, rectangle; the cereal is below the nut, or the nut is above the cereal.

Page 28
1. 13; 2. 18, 19; 3. cube, rectangle; The box is next to the remote control; 4. Check students' answers; 5. Check students' answers.

Page 29
Day 1: Students should circle the set of socks; **Day 2:** ; **Day 3:** light; **Day 4:** 10

Page 30
1. Students should circle the set of caps;
2. •••••; 3. heavy; 4. 16;
5. Students should circle the set of turtles.

Page 31
Day 1: Check students' answers;
Day 2: Students should circle the

set of bags; **Day 3:**
Day 4: 15

Page 32

1. ; 2. Students should circle
the set of hats; 3. ; 4. 11; 5.
Check students' answers.

Page 33
Day 1: short; **Day 2:** 20;
Day 3: Students should circle the
set of mittens; **Day 4:**

Page 34
1. 13; 2. Students should circle the
set of balls; 3. Students should
circle the set of strawberries;
4. ; 5. tall

Page 35

Day 1: ; **Day 2:** 18;
Day 3: Check students' answers;
Day 4: Students should circle the
set of carrots.

Page 36
1. 14; 2. Check students' answers;
3. ; 4. Students should
circle the set of tomatoes;
5.

Page 37
Day 1: Students should circle
the set of walnuts; **Day 2:**
Day 3: light; **Day 4:** 19

Page 38

1. ; 2. heavy; 3. 17;
4. Students should circle the set of
worms; 5. Students should circle
the set of pretzels.

Page 39
Day 1: 12, 13; **Day 2:** Students should circle the set of crayons; **Day 3:** 10, 8; **Day 4:** Check students' answers.

Page 40
1. Students should circle the set of pencils; 2. 10, 5; 3. 13, 14; 4. Check students' answers; 5. 10, 7

Page 41
Day 1: long; **Day 2:** 9; **Day 3:** Students should circle the set of pies; **Day 4:** 10, 3

Page 42
1. Students should circle the set of birds; 2. Students should circle the set of mugs; 3. 10, 4; 4. short; 5. 8

Page 43
Day 1: 10, 2; **Day 2:** 5; **Day 3:** Students should color the ice-cream cone, the party hat, and the traffic cone; **Day 4:** Students should circle the set of balloons.

Page 44
1. Students should color Earth, the ball, and the baseball; 2. 10, 6; 3. Students should circle the set of paper clips; 4. 10, 9; 5. 3

Page 45
Day 1: Check students' answers; **Day 2:** 10, 1; **Day 3:** light; **Day 4:** 10; 11

Page 46
1. heavy; 2. 9, 10; 3. Check students' answers; 4. Check students' answers; 5. 10, 7

Page 47
Day 1: 7, 8; **Day 2:** Check students' answers; **Day 3:** 10, 6; **Day 4:** Students should color the can, the drum, and the roll of paper towels.

Page 48
1. 10, 5; 2. 4, 5; 3. Students should color the gift, the box, and the dice; 4. 10, 1; 5. Check students' answers.

Page 49
Day 1: 5; **Day 2:** 2 + 1 = 3; **Day 3:** 5 + 3 = 8; **Day 4:** Check students' answers.

Page 50
1. 6; 2. 4 + 1 = 5; 3. 4 + 2 = 6; 4. Check students' answers; 5. 9

Answer Key

Page 51
Day 1: apples; Check students' pictures; **Day 2:** Check students' answers; **Day 3:** 1, 2, 3, 2;

Day 4: ☐

Page 52
1. 6 red beads; Check students' pictures; 2. Check students' answers; 3. 2, 4, 3, 2; 4. ◯; 5. 8 seashells; Check students' pictures.

Page 53
Day 1: 3 + 1 = 4; **Day 2:** 10 tables; Check students' pictures; **Day 3:** Check students' answers; **Day 4:** 7

Page 54
1. 3 + 2 = 5; 2. Check students' answers; 3. 7 animals; Check students' pictures; 4. 1 + 1 = 2; 5. 6

Page 55
Day 1: Check students' answers; **Day 2:** 2, 5, 3; **Day 3:** △; **Day 4:** 5 players; Check students' answers.

Page 56
1. Check students' answers; 2. ⬭; 3. 2, 1, 3, 4; 4. Check students' answers; 5. 3 flowers; Check students' pictures.

Page 57
Day 1: Check students' answers; **Day 2:** 7; **Day 3:** 5, 7; **Day 4:** 5 + 2 = 7

Page 58
1. 7, 10; 2. 8; 3. 10, 5; 4. 1 + 3 = 4; 5. Check students' answers.

Page 59
Day 1: Answers will vary. **Day 2:** Check students' answers; **Day 3:** 4 buttons: Check students' pictures; **Day 4:** △

Page 60
1. ⬜; 2. 8 lollipops; Check students' pictures; 3. Check students' answers; 4. Answers will vary; 5. ☐

Page 61
Day 1: 7 – 2 = 5 baseballs; **Day 2:** 7 – 3 = 4; **Day 3:** 7; **Day 4:** Check students' answers.

Page 62
1. Check students' answers; 2. 7 – 3 = 4 baseball gloves; 3. 9; 4. 9 – 1 = 8; 5. 8 – 4 = 4 players

Page 63
Day 1: 6; **Day 2:** 2 forks; Check students' pictures; **Day 3:** Check students' answers; **Day 4:**

Page 64
1. ; 2. 2; 3. 1 canned good; Check students' pictures; 4. Check students' answers; 5. 1

Page 65
Day 1: Check students' answers; **Day 2:** 4 fish; Check students' pictures; **Day 3:** 10 – 5 = 5; **Day 4:** 3

Page 66
1. 5; 2. 5 – 1 = 4; 3. 2 birds; Check students' pictures; 4. Check students' answers; 5. 1 – 1 = 0

Page 67
Day 1: ; **Day 2:** Check students' answers; **Day 3:** 9 hamburgers; Check students' answers; **Day 4:** 10 – 7 = 3

Page 68
1. ; 2. 9 – 5 = 4; 3. Check students' answers; 4. 5 ice-cream cones; Check students' answers; 5. Check students' answers.

Page 69
Day 1: Check students' answers; **Day 2:** 8; **Day 3:** 6 + 3 = 9; **Day 4:** Check students' answers.

Page 70
1. Check students' answers; 2. 9; 3. 5 + 4 = 9; 4. Check students' answers; 5. 7

Page 71
Day 1: Students should draw 3 umbrellas; **Day 2:** Check students' answers; **Day 3:** Answers will vary; **Day 4:** book

Page 72
1. Students should draw 6 flowers; 2. Check students' answers; 3. Answers will vary; 4. table; 5. Check students' answers.

Page 73
Day 1: 8; **Day 2:** Check students' answers; **Day 3:** sphere; **Day 4:** 8 – 3 = 5

Page 74
1. 8 – 6 = 2; 2. Check students'
answers; 3. cylinder; 4. 6;
5. 9 – 4 = 5

Page 75
Day 1: 18; **Day 2:** Students should

circle the set of socks; **Day 3:** ;
Day 4: Students should draw 7
apples.

Page 76
1. Students should draw 8 dots; 2.
10; 3. Students should draw
4 bananas; 4. Students should

circle the set of footballs; 5.

Page 77
Day 1: Check students' answers;
Day 2: 8; **Day 3:** Check students'
answers; **Day 4:** 7 + 0 = 7

Page 78
1. Check students' answers; 2. 6 +
4 = 10; 3. Check students' answers;
4. 5; 5. 5 + 3 = 8

Page 79
Day 1: ladder; **Day 2:** Answers
will vary; **Day 3:** Check students'
answers; **Day 4:** Students should
draw 1 circle.

Page 80
1. the classroom wall; 2. Answers
will vary; 3. Check students'
answers; 4. Students should draw
6 squares; 5. Check students'
answers.

Page 81
Day 1: 15; **Day 2:** Students should
circle the set of rakes; **Day 3:** 3;
Day 4: 6 – 4 = 2

Page 82
1. Students should circle the set of
hats; 2. 3 – 1 = 2; 3. 1; 4. Students
should circle the set of water
drops; 5. 12

Page 83
Day 1: 5 + 3 = 8 turtles;
Day 2: Check students' answers;
Day 3: Students should draw 2
triangles; **Day 4:** cone

Page 84
1. square; 2. Students should draw
6 hands; 3. 7 + 2 = 9 flowers;
4. Check students' answers; 5.
Students should draw
9 rectangles.

Page 85
Day 1: 4, 4; **Day 2:** 17; **Day 3:** 10;
Day 4: 3 + 5 = 8

Page 86
1. 4, 3; 2. 5; 3. 9; 4. 6 + 1 = 7; 5. 11

Page 87
Day 1: Check students' answers;
Day 2: 4 + 4 = 8; **Day 3:** Students
should circle the set of giraffes;
Day 4: 2, 1

Page 88
1. Check students' answers; 2. 1,
0; 3. Students should circle the
zebra; 4. 2, 0; 5. 5 + 5 = 10

 CD-104589 • © Carson-Dellosa